Detroit Red Wings

YEARBOOK

1998-1999

MEMBER OF NATIONAL HOCKEY LEAGUE
Detroit Red Wings

Dear Red Wings fans:

Back-to-back Stanley Cup championships — what a historic time for Detroit hockey!

The thrill of bringing the Stanley Cup back to Detroit for two consecutive years is a dream come true, and we are so appreciative of the unwavering support of everyone in Hockeytown. Your belief in the Wings is an inspiration to our hockey franchise and the National Hockey League.

Very recently, *The Sporting News* named Detroit "The Best Sports City in the U.S." That comes as no surprise to us — we know Detroit sports fans are one of a kind.

Thanks for making last season another incredibly memorable one, and for your continued support for Vladimir Konstantinov and Sergei Mnatsakanov and their families. Their presence at our games was touching for each and every one of us, and we are so happy to see them make progress in their recoveries.

We look forward to sharing another wonderful hockey season with you all!

Best regards,

Mike and Marian Ilitch

Mike and Marian Ilitch

Tim enjoyed his birthday.

Now he's fast asleep.

What shapes and colors can you see in his room?

The end

1998-99 DETROIT RED WING

YEARBOOK

CONTENTS

Produced by CFW Creative Sports, Inc.
Photography by Action Image/Mark Hicks

Management Team

Atanas
ILITCH
VICE PRESIDENT

Chris
ILITCH
VICE PRESIDENT

Jim
DEVELLANO
SENIOR VICE PRESIDENT/
HOCKEY OPERATIONS

Ken
HOLLAND
GENERAL MANAGER

Jim
NILL
ASST. GENERAL MANAGER

Support Staff

John
WHARTON
ATHLETIC THERAPIST
Entering 8th year

Paul
BOYER
EQUIPMENT MANAGER
Entering 5th year

Tim
ABBOTT
ASST. EQUIPMENT MANAGER
Entering 7th year

Wally
CROSSMAN
DRESSING ROOM ASSISTANT
Entering 53rd year

Dr. John Finley, D.O. **TEAM PHYSICIAN**

Dr. David Collon, M.D. **TEAM PHYSICIAN**

Dr. C.J. Regula, D.M.D. **TEAM DENTIST**

Scouting Staff

Dan Belisle	NHL Scout
Jim Nill	Director of Player Development/AHL Scout
Mark Howe	Pro Scout/Minor League Player Development
Joe McDonnell	Eastern Scout
Bruce Haralson	Western Scout
Mark Leach	Eastern, USA, High School & College Scout
Hakan Andersson	Director of European Scouting
Vladimir Havluj	Czech & Slovak Republic Scout
Ruslan Shabanov	Russian Scout
Paul Crowley	Scout
Marty Stein	Scout

HEAD COACH

Born: Montreal, Quebec
9.18.33
Years Coached: 26
Acquired: 6.15.93

Scotty Bowman

Scotty is the winningest coach in NHL history. In a 26 year period, he coached against 34 teams and has a winning record against all of them. He has coached 8 Stanley Cup winning teams. He is the only coach in NHL history to achieve a 60-win season. He did it twice...with Montreal in 1976-77 and with Detroit in 1995-96. He is the all-time leader in almost all important coaching categories. Most regular season games with 1818. Most regular season victories with 1057. Most playoff victories with 194. Highest win percentage with .659. He was named Coach of the Year after the record-breaking 62 victories by the Red Wings in 1995-96.

He knows exactly what it takes to win, what kind of team, what kind of players and what kind of environment.

He created a Red Wing team that was fast and dangerous. He established 4 high performance lines that nullified defensemen all year long. No other team in the NHL was as deep or as balanced as the Red Wings. He seemed to have paced his team during the regular season to have them ready for the playoff march for the Cup. He did, and they were.

William Scott Bowman and his wife Suella, have five children, Alicia, David, Bob, Nancy...and Stanley.
They spend the off-season in suburban Buffalo.

Stats

	Team	Games	Wins	Loses	Ties	Cup Wins
1967-71	St. Louis	238	110	83	45	-
1971-79	Montreal	634	419	110	105	5
1979-87	Buffalo	404	210	134	60	-
1991-93	Pittsburgh	164	95	53	16	1
1993-98	Detroit	378	223	103	52	2

Dave Lewis

Associate Coach

Entering 11th year

Acquired: 11.6.87

Dave Lewis has been a key member of the Red Wing coaching staff for eleven years. He has worked with three different Red Wing coaches. He began with Jacques Demers, continued under Bryan Murray and presently is Associate Coach under Scotty Bowman.

Lewis calls on his 15 years experience as an NHL defenseman to keep the Red Wing team fine-tuned defensively to continue to be one of the best in the NHL season after season. He also does extensive video work, pre-scouting and evaluating opponents.

Dave Lewis is 43 years old. He signed with the Detroit Red Wings as a free agent (no compensation) on July 28, 1986. He joined the Red Wings' coaching staff, immediately after retiring as a player on November 6, 1987 during his 15th NHL season.

Born and raised in Kindersley, SK, Lewis played junior hockey for Saskatoon (WHL) and was the New York Islanders' second pick (33rd overall) in the 1973 Entry Draft. He was selected by Jim Devellano who was the Islanders' chief scout at the time. Lewis made the big pro leap from the junior ranks to the NHL. He never played in the minor leagues.

A milestone in Dave's career as player was his 1000th regular-season game against Philadelphia at the Joe Louis Arena on April 1, 1987. He played a total of 1008 regular season games with the Islanders, Los Angeles, New Jersey and Detroit. He scored 36 goals, 187 assists, and served 953 minutes in the penalty box. He also played in 91 playoff games, with 1 goal, 20 assists and 143 penalty minutes.

Milestones in his coaching career are, of course, the back-to-back Stanley Cup championships and his contribution to establishing one of the greatest teams in NHL history.

Dave and his wife Brenda live in suburban Detroit. They have a son, Ryan and a daughter, Meagan.

The Largest

Harley-Davidson Showroom in The Midwest

Dedicated to Service

Factory Trained Technicians in Our State of the Art Facility

Accessorize

Harley-Davidson Motorcloths, Jewelry, and collectibles

1999 MODELS AVAILABLE NOW!

SUPPLING GREATER DETROIT'S THUNDER

Motown Harley-Davidson & Buell's Mission is to provide top quality motorcycle products and services to the motorcycling public. We have a commitment to quality that creates opportunities for our customers and employees to fulfill their vision. Motown Harley-Davidson & Buell's success is built upon using our products and services to organize our ideas into plans of action. A high level of integrity ensures customer's faith in our business, its employees and Harley-Davidson products.

MOTOWN

MOTOR HARLEY-DAVIDSON CYCLES

TAYLOR, MICHIGAN

WWW.MOTOWNHARLEY.COM

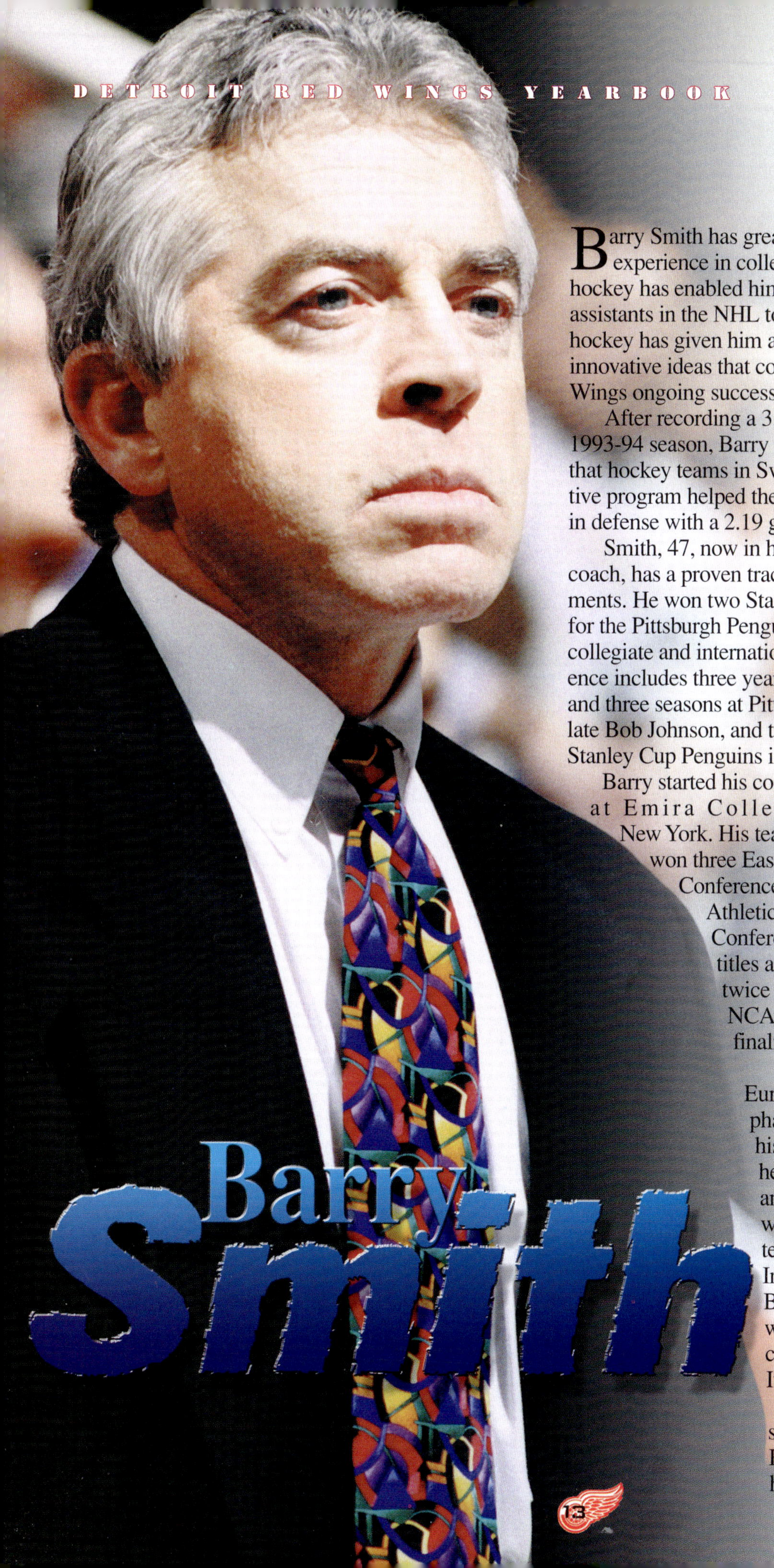

Barry Smith

ASSOCIATE COACH

Entering 6th year

Acquired: 7.28.93

Barry Smith has great depth in coaching. His extensive experience in collegiate, international and professional hockey has enabled him to become one of the top coaching assistants in the NHL today. His extensive knowledge of hockey has given him a solid foundation to implement innovative ideas that continue to contribute to the Red Wings ongoing success.

After recording a 3.24 goals-against-average during the 1993-94 season, Barry introduced the *left-wing-lock system* that hockey teams in Sweden were utilizing. This innovative program helped the Red Wings to lead all NHL teams in defense with a 2.19 goals-against-average.

Smith, 47, now in his sixth season as a Red Wing coach, has a proven track record of coaching accomplishments. He won two Stanley Cup rings as assistant coach for the Pittsburgh Penguins and several championships on collegiate and international competitions. His NHL experience includes three years as an assistant coach at Buffalo and three seasons at Pittsburgh. The first season under the late Bob Johnson, and two years with Scotty Bowman's Stanley Cup Penguins in 1991-92.

Barry started his coaching career in 1975 as head coach at Emira College in New York. His teams won three Eastern Conference Athletic Conference titles and twice were NCAA finalists.

In the European phase of his career, he coached in Sweden from 1981-84 and in Norway from 1984-86. He was assistant coach for the Norway team in the World Championships. In March of 1986, he went to Buffalo as Bowman's assistant. He went to Italy for the 1989 season to coach the *Alleghe* club and the Italian National team.

Barry and his wife Mary have a son, Ryan, and a daughter, Molly. He spends the off-seasons in his hometown of Buffalo, New York.

no. 4

DEFENSE

6’6”’

235 lbs

Shoots Right

Born: Cologne, West Germany

6.24.65

Last Amateur Club:

Koln -West Germany

Years Pro: 13

Acquired:

Signed as a free agent 7.6.98

Uwe adds more than his outstanding size to the Red Wing team, he brings with him experience and versatility. And, he's got a good low shot from the points. Huge. Intimidating. Deceptive. Effective.

He carries the puck well out of his own zone. He will fill a void that was left by the departure of Bob Rouse and Dmitri Mironov. He will be teamed up with six-foot-three Anders Eriksson to create a defensive *dynamic duo* that could be down-right scary on the ice.

This is not his first Stanley Cup Team. He scored the cup-winning goal for the Colorado Avalanche in 1996. Last season, he led the Avalanche in plus/minus with a plus-21, which tied him for 14th in NHL with his new ice-mate Anders.

He was named an NHL All-Star in 1991, the season in which he scored a career-high of 12 goals and 32 assists for 44 points.

During his 12 seasons in the NHL, Krupp has played in 695 regular season games, scored 66 goals and 209 assists for 275 points. He was originally drafted by Buffalo in the 1983 Entry Draft. He was their 13th choice and 214th overall. He was traded to the New York Islanders in 1991. After 2-1/2 seasons with New York, he was traded to Quebec for one season, and then to the Colorado Avalanche in 1995.

Uwe spent the summer rehabilitating and running hockey clinics in Aspen, Colorado Springs, Greely and Steamboat. He vacationed with his family in Hawaii and Fairbanks, Alaska. He owns and races sled dogs. He has two sons, Bjorn and Cedric.

STATS

		SEASON	GP	G	A	PTS	PM
NHL	BUF	1986-87	26	1	4	5	23
AHL			42	3	19	22	50
NHL	BUF	1987-88	75	2	9	11	151
NHL	BUF	1988-89	70	5	13	18	55
NHL	BUF	1989-90	74	3	20	23	85
NHL	BUF	1990-91	74	12	32	44	66
NHL	BUF	1991-92	8	2	0	2	6
NHL	NY I		59	6	29	35	43
NHL	NY I	1992-93	80	9	29	38	67
NHL	NY I	1993-94	41	7	14	21	30
GERMANY		1994-95	5	1	2	3	6
NHL	QUE	1995	44	6	17	23	20
NHL	COL	1995-96	6	0	3	3	4
NHL	COL	1996-97	60	4	17	21	48
NHL	COL	1997-98	78	9	22	31	38

Uwe Krupp

no. 5

DEFENSE

6'2"
190 lbs
Shoots Left
Born: Vasteras, Sweden
4.28.70
Last Amateur Club:
Vasteras (Sweden)
Years Pro: 7
Acquired: 3rd choice,
53rd overall in 1989 Draft

Nicklas Lidstrom

Nicklas is the Red Wings' secret weapon. A silent superstar. He is one of the most underrated players in the NHL. Calm. Quiet. Level-headed. Well-mannered. Outstanding on defense and a surprising scorer. The Red Wings rely on his exceptional performance on the power play or penalty kill. He led all defensemen in scoring last season with 59 points (17 goals-42 assists). He scored 6 goals in 22 post season games. He averaged more than 30 minutes ice time per game.

He was named one of Sweden's top three players in the 1990 World Junior Championships. He played in the 1991 Canada Cup with Sweden and the 1991 and 1994 World Champions, helping Sweden win a gold medal in 1991.

He made his NHL debut in October of 1991. He made the All Rookie Team and was runner-up for the Calder Trophy. Among all NHL rookies, he ranked first in assists, first in plus-minus and tied for third in scoring. He also set the Red Wing record for assists by a rookie defenseman.

In 1995, Nicklas was second in scoring for the NHL playoffs and tied the club record for assists by a blueliner. He also scored his career best 67 points and played in his first NHL All-Star Game.

He was second on the team in the 1997 playoffs with +12 and scored a goal in the Stanley Cup clinching game. He scored 19 points (6 goals-13 assists) in the 1998 playoffs, including the game-winning goal against Washington in Game 1.

Nicklas, his wife Annika and their 2 sons, return to Lidstrom's hometown of Vasteras, Sweden where he enjoys tennis and golf in the off season.

STATS

		SEASON	*GP*	*G*	*A*	*PTS*	*PM*
SWEDEN		1988-89	19	0	2	2	4
SWEDEN		1989-90	39	8	8	16	14
SWEDEN		1990-91	38	4	19	23	2
NHL	DET	1991-92	80	11	49	60	22
NHL	DET	1992-93	84	7	34	41	28
NHL	DET	1993-94	84	10	46	56	26
NHL	DET	1995	43	10	16	26	6
NHL	DET	1995-96	81	17	50	67	20
NHL	DET	1996-97	79	15	42	57	30
NHL	DET	1997-98	80	17	42	59	18

no. 8

CENTER

5'9"

170 lbs

Shoots Left

Born: Voskresensk, Russia

12.3.60

Last Amateur Club:

Central Red Army (Russia)

Years Pro: 8

Acquired: Obtained 10.24.95

from San Jose for Ray Sheppard

Igor Larionov is a former hero of the Russian National Team and a charter member of the Russian Five. His nickname is The Professor. And off the ice, he looks like a professor, you wouldn't expect him to be a hockey player. Highly skilled. Highly intelligent. Great vision. Unequaled commitment. Igor is a master of getting an opponent out of position. He excels at passing the puck to the open man. He always plays with the Russian philosophy that anything but winning is a failure.

In the first Stanley Cup Championship season, Igor scored 54 points, with 12 goals and 42 assists. He added another 4 goals and 8 assists in the playoffs, including a game winning goal.

Larionov was a true Russian hero. He was a veteran of many international competitions with the Soviet National Team, which included capturing gold medals in both the 1984 and 1988 Winter Olympics.

He was the center of the famous KLM line with Vladimir Krutov and Sergei Makarov during the 1980's. Igor was named to five All-Star teams and earned the Soviet Player of the Year honors in 1988.

He was drafted by Vancouver in 1985 and then acquired by San Jose in the waiver Draft in 1992. He played three seasons for the Sharks and tied their all-time career plus/minus record at 17. He joined the Red Wings in 1995. In his first year, he set a career record for points (71), and was tied for fourth in club scoring, assists and power play goals.

In the first championship season, Igor finished fifth on the club in scoring(54), tied for second with assists (42), scored two goals in the Conference Finals, and two other two-point games in the playoffs. He along with his Russian teammate Fetisov were such an inspiration to the team that Stevie Yzerman handed the Stanley Cup to them during the 1997 victory celebration. In the 1998 playoffs, Igor scored 13 points which included 5 game-winning assists to prove his willingness to do whatever it takes for the team.

Off-season, Igor loves to travel to Europe, loves red wines and loves to spend time with his wife, Elena and two daughters, Alyonka and Dianna, and new son Igor.

STATS

	SEASON	GP	G	A	PTS	PM
SOVIET	1987-88	51	25	32	57	54
SOVIET	1988-89	31	15	12	27	22
NHL VAN	1989-90	74	17	27	44	20
NHL VAN	1990-91	64	13	21	34	14
NHL VAN	1991-92	72	21	44	65	54
SWITZ	1992-93	24	10	19	29	44
NHL S J	1993-94	60	18	38	56	40
NHL S J	1995	33	4	20	24	14
NHL S J	1995-96	4	1	1	2	0
NHL DET		69	21	50	71	34
NHL DET	1996-97	64	12	42	54	26
NHL DET	1997-98	69	8	39	47	3

Igor Larionov

no. 11

RIGHT WING

6'1"
196 lbs
Shoots Right
Born: Sherbrooke, Quebec
2.3.76
Last Amateur Club:
Sherbrooke Faucons
Years Pro: 3
Acquired: 2nd choice,
49 overall in 1994 Entry Draft

Mathieu is a skater, a very fast skater. He should play a more important role for the Red Wings this season. Young. Eager. Energetic. Speed. And more speed. He can play any position and loves the game. His nickname is Dandy. He scored his career high in points (17), assists (12) and matched his career high of 5 goals. He got his first career playoff point against Phoenix in Game 2 by scoring a power play goal. He also registered a career-best four-game scoring streak.

Before joining the Red Wings, Mathieu played with the Sherbrooke Faucons, where he led in goals, assists and points in both 1994 and 1995 seasons.

He was ninth in amateur league scoring overall.

Dandy was Detroit's second choice in the 1994 Entry Draft and made his NHL debut at Edmonton on October 8, 1995.

His first NHL point was a power play goal on November 2 at Boston. His first assist came in the same month against Los Angeles. His first career two-goal score came in December 1995 at Montreal.

Mathieu was the youngest player on the Red Wings team during the 1996-97 season. He had a two game point streak in January and two other two-point streaks during the regular season. Mathieu also assisted on one game-winning goal and played in his first Stanley Cup Championship.

He is single and spends his off-season in his hometown of Sherbrooke when he's not playing with the Red Wings charity softball team.

STATS

	SEASON	GP	G	A	PTS	PM
QMJHL	1993-94	67	17	36	53	67
QMJHL	1994-95	67	37	70	107	76
NHL DET	1995-96	34	5	7	12	6
NHL DET	1996-97	65	3	9	12	28
NHL DET	1997-98	68	5	12	17	43

Mathieu Dandenault

no. 13

<u>LEFT WING</u>

5'10"

195 lbs

Shoots Left

Born: Voskresensk, Russia

5.3.72

Last Amateur Club:

Central Red Army (Russia)

Years Pro: 7

Acquired: 2nd choice, 45th overall in 1990 Draft

Vyacheslav is the little player who makes big plays. He has an inherent knack for being in the right place at the right time. He loves to score goals. Quiet. Skilled. Tough. Courageous. He plays with purpose, poise and discipline. His teammates call him Kozzie.

Kozzie was a playoff star last year. He scored one game winning goal against Phoenix, 1 game-winning goal and 2 game-winning assists against St. Louis, and 2 game-winning goals against Dallas.

Kozzie showed his early promise when he starred in the 1989-90 World Junior Championships, and he was named Rookie of the Year in the Soviet Elite League. He helped the Russian team win the gold medal in the 1990 Goodwill Games in Seattle. He also helped win the 1991 and 1994 World Championships and the 1991 Canada Cup. He was drafted by the Red Wings in 1990. In 1993, he posted his career-high eight-game point streak.

In the 1995 playoffs, he scored the game-winning goal of Game 5 against Chicago, at 2:25 of the second overtime period to clinch the Western Conference title. In the 1995-96 season, he tied a career-high of 73 points and was tied for second on the team for goals(36). In the 1996-97 season, Vyacheslav scored the game-winning, power-play goal in triple overtime on May 4 against Anaheim. He finished 3rd on the team in goals (23) and was tied for second in game- winning goals. Kozzie's impressive 14 point contribution in last year's Stanley Cup repeat is a prime example of his poise under pressure. He always seems to show up at the right moment, late in the game to help his team.

Kozlov is single and lives in suburban Detroit.

He plays on the Red Wings charity softball team in the off-season and usually visits his hometown of Voskresensk, Russia.

STATS

	SEASON	GP	G	A	PTS	PM
SOVIET	1987-88	2	0	0	0	0
SOVIET	1988-89	13	0	1	1	2
SOVIET	1989-90	45	14	12	26	38
SOVIET	1990-91	45	11	13	24	46
SOVIET	1991-92	11	6	5	11	12
NHL DET	1991-92	7	0	2	2	2
NHL DET	1992-93	17	4	1	5	14
AHL		45	23	36	59	54
NHL DET	1993-94	77	34	39	73	50
AHL		3	0	1	1	15
NHL DET	1994-95	46	13	20	33	45
NHL DET	1995-96	82	36	37	73	70
NHL DET	1996-97	75	23	22	45	46
NHL DET	1997-98	80	25	27	52	46

Slava Kozlov

no. 14

LEFT WING

6'3"

215 lbs

Shoots Right

Born: Mimico, ON.

1.23.69

Last Amateur Club:

London (OHL)

Years Pro: 11

Acquired: Traded by

Hartford,10.9.96

Brendan Shanahan is a big shooter. He loves to score. He is a two-time 50 goal forward. His slap shot is incredible. He takes no time to shoot it. Big. Powerful. Competitive. Focused. Shanny's style of play is very physical and always an explosive scoring threat.

Another 1998 playoff highlight was when he beat the legendary Grant Fuhr at 11:12 seconds of the second overtime for a 3-2 victory against the St. Louis (Black and) Blues.

Brendan played for Canada in the 1986 World Junior Championships in Czechoslovakia. He was New Jersey's first pick in the 1987 entry draft, second overall. He signed as a free agent with St. Louis in July 1991. He made his NHL debut in October of 1987 and he scored his first career goal in November of 1987. It was a game-winning goal. And so was his second NHL goal.

He scored his first career hat trick in 1989 to accent an impressive 30-goal season. In the 1992-93 season he broke the 50 goal mark for the first time.

The following year he scored his career highs in goals (52), assists (50), points (102) and penalty minutes (211).

In 1994, he also made first team NHL All-Star and scored two goals in the All-Star game. Shanny was named NHL Player of the Month for April and led the NHL in hat tricks, total shots, and shorthanded goals. During the 1995-96 season, he led the Whalers in goals, points and power play goals. He was voted a starter for the 1996 All-Star Game and played for Team Canada in the 1996 World Cup of Hockey.

He emphasized his start with the Red Wings in October 1996 with his first Red Wing point and his 600th career point. He finished the 1996-97 season in overall team scoring, first in goals, second in assists, second in plus/minus and first in power play goals, shorthanded goals and game-winning goals. He also recorded back-to-back hat tricks that season.

He finished last season leading the Red Wings with 28 goals, 15 power play goals and 9 game-winning goals. He had 9 playoff points, 5 goals and 4 assists. Recently married, Brendan and his wife reside in suburban Detroit.

STATS	SEASON	GP	G	A	PTS	PM
NHL NJ	1987-88	65	7	19	26	131
NHL NJ	1988-89	68	22	28	50	115
NHL NJ	1989-90	73	30	42	72	137
NHL NJ	1990-91	75	29	37	66	141
NHL STL	1991-92	80	33	36	69	171
NHL STL	1992-93	71	51	43	94	174
NHL STL	1993-94	81	52	50	102	211
GERMANY	1994-95	3	5	3	8	4
NHL STL	1995	45	20	21	41	136
NHL HFD	1995-96	74	44	34	78	125
NHL HFD	1996-97	2	1	0	1	0
NHL DET	1996-97	79	46	41	87	131
NHL DET	1997-98	75	28	29	57	154

Brendan Shanahan

no. 17

Right Wing

5'10"

185 lbs

Shoots Right

Born: New Haven, CT, 6.12.64

Last Amateur Club: Boston College (HE)

Years Pro: 12

Acquired: Obtained in NHL Waiver Draft 1.18.95

Doug Brown

Doug Brown is a true plugger. A gritty American winger who turns on the offense like a light switch. Intelligent. Skilled. Fluid. Adaptable. Brownie is a strong Red Wing utility player. He can play the point on the power play or the forward positions on the scoring line or checking line.

He scored two key playoff goals in the run for the repeat last year. With blood on his red beard he scored the tying goal in Game 2 of the Finals to send it into overtime.

Doug comes from an American family with strong hockey genes. His brother, Greg, also played in the NHL. Doug played four seasons while at Boston College and made the Hockey East First All-Star Team in both his junior and senior years. He earned a place on TEAM USA in 1986 and 1989, and 1991 World Championships and on the 1991 Canada Cup team.

Brownie has never been drafted. He started his NHL career as a free agent and signed with New Jersey in 1986. During his first full season (1987-88), he was named the Devils Top Rookie. He played with the Devils in the 1988 conference final and scored the first playoff overtime goal.

Doug was signed as a free agent by the Pittsburgh Penguins in 1993 and scored his career highs in goals (18), assists (37) and total points (55).

He joined the Red Wing organization in 1995 via the NHL waiver draft. In the 1996-97 conference finals against Colorado, Doug assisted on two game- winning goals, and he scored three goals in three games in the series against Anaheim. He scored two goals in the final game of the Stanley Cup series last year to cap off the Red Wings sweep repeat.

Doug and his wife Maureen have two sons and two daughters, and spend the off-season in Harrison, New York, playing golf and tennis.

STATS

		SEASON	GP	G	A	PTS	PM
NHL	NJ	1987-88	70	14	11	25	20
AHL			2	0	2	2	2
NHL	NJ	1988-89	63	15	10	25	15
AHL			4	1	4	5	0
NHL	NJ	1989-90	69	14	20	34	16
NHL	NJ	1990-91	58	14	16	30	4
NHL	NJ	1991-92	71	11	17	28	27
NHL	NJ	1992-93	15	0	5	5	2
AHL			25	11	17	28	8
NHL	PIT	1993-94	77	18	37	55	18
NHL	DET	1995	45	9	12	21	16
NHL	DET	1995-96	62	12	15	27	4
NHL	DET	1996-97	49	6	7	13	8
NHL	DET	1997-98	80	19	23	42	12

no. 18

Left Wing

6'0"

190lbs

Shoots Right

Born: Guelph, ON

12.22.72

Last Amateur Club:

Owen Sound (OHL)

Years Pro: 6

Acquired: Traded by

Edmonton, 3.20.96

Kirk Maltby

Kirk Maltby is a banger. He loves to hit. He loves to get under the opponents' skin. He is the infinite pest. Tough. Rugged. Aggressive. Pugnacious. Malts is a member in good standing of the Grind Line. When he gets hit, he hits back harder. He loves to level his opponents or give a sneaky jab to the goalie as he passes the crease.

Kirk posted his career best in goals, assists and points last season. He produced 3 goals and 1 assist in the playoffs and did his part in crumbling the Bulin Wall.

He started hockey with the Owen Sound Platers and was named Rookie of the Year in 1989-90. He was chosen Most Valuable Player in both the 1990-91 and 1991-92 seasons. His final amateur season he was named team captain, and also played in the CHL East- West All-Star Challenge. He played with the Cape Breton Oilers in 1992-93 and helped them win the AHL Calder Cup.

He scored his first NHL goal in his debut with Edmonton in October 1993. In the 1994-95 season he finished 12th in scoring, eighth in goals and tied for first in shorthanded goals. Malts played his first game as a Red Wing in March 1996. He scored his first goal in April against Winnipeg. His first career NHL playoff goal came on April 27, 1997 in St. Louis. He scored 5 goals in the playoffs, including his first career two-goal game against Colorado. He experienced his first Stanley Cup Championship with the Red Wings in 1997. In the 1998 playoffs, he scored 3 goals and 1 assist in helping the Red Wings to a repeat championship performance.

During a game, Malts can be aggravating enough to provoke the entire bench of the opposing team into a tirade. Off the ice, he is quiet, low-keyed and enjoys being with his teammates. He is single and enjoys softball in his free time.

Stats

		SEASON	GP	G	A	PTS	PM
OHL		1989-90	61	12	15	27	90
OHL		1990-91	66	34	32	66	100
OHL		1991-92	64	50	41	91	99
AHL		1992-93	73	22	23	45	130
NHL	EDM	1993-94	68	11	8	19	74
NHL	EDM	1995	47	8	3	11	49
NHL	EDM	1995-96	49	2	6	8	61
AHL		1995-96	4	1	2	3	6
NHL	DET		6	1	0	1	6
NHL	DET	1996-97	66	3	5	8	75
NHL	DET	1997-98	65	14	9	23	89

no. 19

CENTER

5’10”

185 lbs

Shoots Right

Born: Cranbrook, BC.

5.9.65

Last Amateur Club:

Peteborough Petes (OHL)

Years Pro: 15

Acquired: 1st choice.

4th overall in 1983 Draft

Steve Yzerman

Steve won the Conn Smythe trophy as the most valuable player of the 1998 playoffs. Highly skilled. Tough. Relentless. Always hungry for a win. A true team leader. His teammates call him Silk, because there's nobody smoother on the ice. Drafted by the Red Wings in 1983, he was named Top Rookie by The Sporting News magazine and scored club rookie records in both goals and total points. In 1986, Steve was named captain of the Red Wing team. At age 21, he was the youngest captain in Detroit team history.

The 1988-89 season was mile-stone year for Steve. He set club records in goals, assists and points and ranked third overall in the NHL in each category.

He also became one of only four players in NHL history to get 150 or more points. He scored 65 goals that year and followed with 62 goals in the 1989-90 season to become one of only six players in history to accomplish this scoring feat. He was second in the NHL in goals scored that year.

In 1993, Stevie Y joined the 1000 point club. The following season, he scored his 500th career goal, becoming the 22nd player in NHL history to score that many goals.

The 1996-97 season was a year of milestones for Steve. He played his 1000th career game. He scored his 1300th career point and his 800th career assist. His 3-point November effort against San Jose moved up to second place on the all-time Red Wings point list.

But Stevie's most important goal of the 1997 season, or maybe even his 15-year career was in the second playoff game against Colorado, when he skated behind the net and shoved it in off goalie, Patrick Roy's leg. It was the turning point of his team's 42- year quest for the cup.

Leading his team to back-to-back Stanley Cup championships, Stevie-Y has earned a special place in Red Wing history and the hearts of hockey's greatest fans.

Whatever off time Steve doesn't spend with his wife, Lisa and their two children, might be filled with an unannounced visit to the children's floor at a local hospital.

STATS

		SEASON	GP	G	A	PTS	PM
NHL	DET	1987-88	64	50	52	102	44
NHL	DET	1988-89	80	65	90	155	61
NHL	DET	1989-90	79	62	65	127	79
NHL	DET	1990-91	80	51	57	108	34
NHL	DET	1991-92	79	45	58	103	64
NHL	DET	1992-93	84	58	79	137	44
NHL	DET	1993-94	58	24	58	82	36
NHL	DET	1995	47	12	26	38	40
NHL	DET	1995-96	80	36	59	95	64
NHL	DET	1996-97	81	22	63	85	78
NHL	DET	1997-98	75	24	45	69	46

no. 20

RIGHT WING

5'11"

215 lbs

Shoots Right

Born: Ville Ste-Pierre, Quebec, 9.12.73

Last Amateur Club: Laval Titians (QMJHL)

*Years Pro:*7

Acquired: 1st choice, 10th overall in 1991 Draft

Martin is a grinder, turned goal-scorer. He loves playing the big games. Thick. Strong. Powerful. Bulldog. He's a hard-slamming winger and big banger. His fiery style of play makes his presence on the ice of true concern to the opponents. Whenever Martin is on the ice, menace and mayhem are sure to follow.

His disruptive style of play-breaking played a vital role in the Red Wings championship repeat. And so did his 3 game-winning assists and one game-winning goal.

Martin played with the Laval Titans for four amateur seasons and scored 338 points in 195 games.

He was named to the first All-Star Team in the Quebec Major Junior League in 1989-90 and to the second All- Star Team in 1990-91. He was first choice by the Red Wings in the 1991 Entry Draft, and saw post season action with the Adirondack Calder Cup Championship team in 1992. He made his NHL debut against Toronto in October of '92. He had an assist in his NHL playoff debut on April 26, 1992 against Minnesota. Martin also played in the 1995 AHL All-Star Game.

Martin amassed his career best of 33 points during the 1996-97 season. He followed that up with a new career best of 34 points with 15 goals and 19 assists during the 1997-98 regular season. In the post season, Martin scored two power play goals and one short-handed goal in the St. Louis series. He had playoff game-winning assists against Phoenix, Dallas and Washington. And he scored the game-winning goal against Washington in the final Stanley Cup game.

He scored 9 goals and 6 assists for a total of 15 playoff points to help his teammates keep the Cup in Detroit.

In the off-season, Martin and his wife, Tania and son, Guyot return to his hometown near Montreal. Martin stays in shape by lifting weights and enjoying other summer sports.

STATS		SEASON	GP	G	A	PTS	PM
QMJHL		1989-90	65	42	54	96	77
QMJHL		1990-91	64	44	54	98	66
NHL	DET	1991-92	4	0	1	1	5
QMJHL			31	25	30	55	81
NHL	DET	1992-93	3	0	0	0	5
AHL			8	1	2	3	9
QMJHL			35	38	51	89	41
NHL	DET	1993-94	50	8	8	16	55
AHL			28	25	21	46	47
AHL		1994-95	39	29	16	45	80
NHL	DET	1995	39	4	6	10	73
NHL	DET	1995-96	58	6	3	9	93
NHL	DET	1996-97	78	16	17	33	167
NHL	DET	1997-98	79	15	19	34	106

Martin Lapointe

no. 25

RIGHT WING

6'1"

215 lbs

Shoots Right

Born: Burnaby, BC.

4.1.72

Last Amateur Club:

Belleville Bulls (OHL)

Years Pro: 5

Acquired: 2nd choice.

46th overall in 1992 draft

Darren McCarty is a hard-nosed right-winger that loves the camera, the fame, the glory. Fans can always get to him. He loves Hockeytown fans. But he loves bone- crushing hockey even more. Fearless. Determined. Combative. Rugged. He will support his teammates to the end. Big Mac has big hockey strength and true grit. Not known as a big scorer, when he scored the game-winning, cup-clinching goal in the 1997 Stanley Cup final game, his teammates on the bench wondered who crawled into his uniform.

Mac started his hockey career with the Belleville Bulls in 1990, and in the 1991-92 season, he led the OHL in goals with 55 goals, 72 assists, 127 points in 65 games. He played one season with the Adirondack Wings before joining the Red Wings as their second choice in the 1992 draft.

His NHL debut was against Winnipeg on October 5, 1993. His first point was an assist against Los Angeles on October 8th. His first goal was on October 21st against Winnipeg. Mac scored his first playoff goal in his NHL playoff debut against San Jose on April 18, 1994.

In 1995, Darren had his first two-goal game, and his first two-power play goal game, against Winnipeg. During the 1996-97 season, he achieved his career high of 49 points and finished sixth in overall team scoring. He was fifth on the club with goals (19).

As a charter member of the Grind Line that scored three goals in Game 1 of the 1998 playoffs, he helped destroy the Bulin Wall and set a tough, new Grind Line standard for the playoffs.

He had a total of 11 playoff points with 3 goals and 8 assists. He helped to establish an awesome physical presence on the ice that kept playoff opponents off their game, and the Red Wings on to a repeat.

Darren, his wife Cheryl, son Griffin, and daughter Emerson live in suburban Detroit. Off-season, he plays in the Red Wings charity softball games, plays an active role in the Make-A-Wish Foundation and has been honored by the Royal Canadian Mounted Police for his assistance in juvenile drug prevention programs.

STATS

		SEASON	GP	G	A	PTS	PM
OHL		1990-91	60	30	37	67	151
OHL		1991-92	65	55	72	127	177
AHL		1992-93	73	17	19	36	278
NHL	DET	1993-94	67	9	17	26	181
NHL	DET	1995	31	5	8	13	88
NHL	DET	1995-96	63	15	14	29	158
NHL	DET	1996-97	68	19	30	49	126
NHL	DET	1997-98	71	15	22	37	157

Darren McCarty

1997-1998 Detroit Red Wings

First Row, from left: Chris Osgood, Kevin Hodson, Sergei Mnatsakanov, Senior Vice-President Jim Devellano, General Manager Ken Holland, Vice-President Atanas Ilitch (Conn Smythe Trophy), Owner/Secretary-Treasurer Marian Ilitch, Owner Mike Ilitch, Captain Steve Yzerman (Stanley Cup), Head Coach Scotty Bowman, Associate Coach Barry Smith, Associate Coach Dave Lewis (Clarence Campbell Bowl), Asst. General Manager Don Waddell, Vladimir Konstantinov, Brendan Shanahan, Norm Maracle.

STANLEY CUP CHAMPIONS

SECOND ROW, FROM LEFT: DRESSING ROOM ASST. WALLY CROSSMAN, ATHLETIC TRAINER JOHN WHARTON, MASSEUR BOB HUDDLESTON, DRESSING ROOM ASST. ART MNATSAKANOV, GOALTENDING CONSULTANT JIM BEDARD, DARRYL LAPLANTE, BRENT GILCHRIST, MARTIN LAPOINTE, TOMAS HOLMSTROM, DARREN MCCARTY, JOE KOCUR, KRIS DRAPER, KIRK MALTBY, DOUG BROWN, IGOR LARIONOV, VYACHESLAV KOZLOV, VIACHESLAV FETISOV, NHL SCOUT DAN BELISLE, VICE-PRESIDENT CHRISTOPHER ILITCH, EQUIPMENT MANAGER PAUL BOYER, ASST. EQUIP MANAGER TIM ABBOTT, DRESSING ROOM ASST. JOHNNY REMEJES.

THIRD ROW, FROM LEFT: DMITRI MIRONOV, MIKE KNUBLE, MATHIEU DANDENAULT, ANDERS ERIKSSON,

Miller Time
Lite
WINGS FANS ARE ALWAYS SAYING,
"I wish I could make better confetti."
NOW YOU CAN! TEAR UP THIS AD ALONG THE LINES AND THROW IT IN THE AIR WHEN THE RED WINGS SCORE.
MILLER LITE: THE HOCKEY BEER FOR HOCKEYTOWN.™
©1998 Miller Brewing Co. Milwaukee, WI. www.millerlite.com
THINK WHEN YOU DRINK

Olympia entertainment
Everything's waiting for you!
70th ANNIVERSARY FOX THEATRE
Rockers DETROIT
The Second City
Joe Louis Arena
COBO Arena
DETROIT ZOO SERVICES
Olympia restaurant group
THE CENTER OF GLENS FALLS
www.olympiaentertainment.com • www.detroitredwings.com

no. 26

RIGHT WING

6'0"

222 lbs

Shoots Right

Born: Calgary, AB

12.21.64

Last Amateur Club:

Saskatoon (WHL)

Years Pro: 14

Acquired: Signed as free agent

12.28.96

Joey Kocur is a seasoned veteran. He's been there, did that. He won a Stanley Cup with the Rangers in 1994. Tough. Leader. Organizer. Experienced. He is also known as The Enforcer...and is quite adept at giving the opponents an ocassional face wash.

Last year, they were calling him Mr. Playoffs. He scored 4 goals in the post season as compared to 6 goals for the regular season.

Joe originally joined the Detroit Red Wings in 1983. He played 5 full seasons and accumulated 111 points, 1,714 penalty minutes in 399 games played.
He scored his career highs in goals(16), assists (20) and points (36) in the 1989-90 season as a Red Wing.

He then played with the New York Rangers for 5 seasons. Kocur was re-signed as a free agent in 1996, and he played the first game of the 1996-97 season for Detroit against Dallas on January 3. This was his 400th game as a Red Wing.

He scored his first goal of the year on February 6 against Vancouver and netted the game-winning goal on March 15 against San Jose. Joey also assisted on the game-tying goal on April 1st against St. Louis.

He launched the sweep of Philadelphia with a goal in game one of the 1997 Stanley Cup finals and assisted on the game-winning goal on June 3 at Philadelphia.

In last year's playoffs he scored his first two- goal game of the season in Game 1 against the wiley Coyotes. He scored two game winning goals during the regular season.

Joe, his wife Kristin and daughter Kendall live in suburban Detroit. Joe runs a hockey school and is an avid golfer.

STATS

		SEASON	GP	G	A	PTS	PM
NHL	DET	1987-88	63	7	7	14	263
NHL	DET	1988-89	60	9	9	18	213
NHL	DET	1989-90	71	16	20	36	268
NHL	DET	1990-91	52	5	4	9	253
NHL	NYR		5	0	0	0	36
NHL	NYR	1991-92	51	7	4	11	121
NHL	NYR	1992-93	65	3	6	9	131
NHL	NYR	1993-94	71	2	1	3	129
NHL	NYR	1995	48	1	2	3	71
NHL	NYR	1995-96	38	1	2	3	49
NHL	VAN		7	0	1	1	19
IHL		1996-97	5	1	1	2	24
NHL	DET	1996-97	34	2	1	3	70
NHL	DET	1997-98	63	6	5	11	92

Joe Kocur

no. 27

DEFENSE

6'2"

225 lbs

Shoots Right

Born: Windsor, ON.

1.17.73

Last Amateur Club:

University of Michigan (CCHA)

Years Pro: 4

Acquired: Obtaines 6.11.93

from Winnipeg

Aaron Ward

Aaron is the Red Wings most physical player. Big. Strong. Hard-hitting. Rugged. Sometimes, even down right nasty. His teammates call him Wardo. He did not play in the playoffs last season but he scored 5 goals and 5 assists in 52 regular season games which registered as his career best in goals, assists, points and games played.

He spent three years playing hockey at the University of Michigan. Then, he played three years with the Adirondack Wings amassing a total of 20 goals, 46 assists and 307 penalty minutes in 208 games. He became a Red Wing in 1993 and scored his first career NHL goal on October 8 in Anaheim.

The 1996-97 was his first full season with Detroit. He scored his first goal of the season on November 4 against Hartford. His first assist came on a short-handed goal against Phoenix on November 18. That started a three-game point streak which ended November 23.

Wardo made his first career NHL playoff appearance on April 18 against St. Louis which led to his first Stanley Cup Championship with the Red Wings.

Aaron and his wife, Kelly spend the off-season in suburban Detroit. Aaron plays on the Red Wings charity softball team and is the Police Athletic League (PAL) representative for the team. He and former teammate Jamie Pushor put on a clinic for the PAL youth hockey team.

Stats

		SEASON	GP	G	A	PTS	PM
CCHA	UM	1990-91	46	8	11	19	126
CCHA	UM	1991-92	42	7	12	19	64
CCHA	UM	1992-93	30	5	8	13	73
CDN	NAT'L		4	0	0	0	8
NHL	DET	1993-94	5	1	0	1	4
AHL			58	4	12	16	87
AHL		1994-95	76	11	24	35	87
NHL	DET		1	0	1	1	2
AHL		1995-96	74	5	10	15	133
NHL	DET	1996-97	49	2	5	7	52
NHL	DET	1997-98	52	5	5	10	47

no. 28

DEFENSE

6'4"'

204 lbs

Shoots Left

Born: Novosibirsk, Russia

3.9.76

Last Amateur Club:

Moscow Dynamos

Years Pro: 3

Golubovsky is a strong and talented rookie with something to prove to the coaches, his teammates and himself. He is compelled to grind with the grinders. Bang with the bangers. Check with the checkers. Skate with the skaters. And win with the winners. He should see more play this season guarding the rear. Fresh. Young. Big. Tough. Yan wants more ice time and he's willing to do whatever it takes to get it.

When Yan was only 17 years old, he played for the Russian Penguins who toured North America during the 1993-94 season. He became the youngest player ever to suit up for the Adirondack Wings on September 30, 1994. He was 18 years, 6 months and 21 days old.

He played for Adirondack in the AHL for three seasons and averaged 14 points a season. He scored his first point of the 1997-98 season for Adirondack on October 11 against Saint John. His first goal of the season came at home against Albany on November 22.

He was called to join the Red Wings in December and made his NHL debut. Yan played in 12 NHL games and scored 2 points. He returned to the Adirondack Wings in January and had 4 assists in a February game against Albany. He missed eight games due to an injury and scored an assist on his first game back.

Yan's size and talent can potentially add even more depth to the best defense in hockey today. And Hockeytown fans are anxiously waiting for the chance to yell ...
Go Go Go-lubovsky.

STATS

	SEASON	GP	G	A	PTS	PM
MOSCOW CIS	1993-94	10	0	1	1	-
AHL	1994-95	57	4	2	6	39
AHL	1995-96	71	5	16	21	97
AHL	1996-97	62	2	11	13	67
AHL	1997-98	52	1	15	16	57
NHL DET		12	0	2	2	6

Yan Golubovsky

no. 30

GOALIE

5'11"

180lbs

Catches Left

Born: Peace River, AB

11.26.72

Last Amateur Club: Seattle Thunderbirds, (WHL)

Years Pro: 5

Acquired: 3rd choice, 54th overall in 1991 entry Draft

Chris Osgood's cup-winning performance has finally earned the respect of the goalie-tough Hockeytown fans who compare every Red Wing goalie to Terry Sawchuck. Quick. Agile. Competitive. Intelligent. Resilient. Ozzie is the Red Wings' Ace In The Hole. His ability to instantly forget a bad goal, like Langenbrunner's 88 foot game-winning bouncer in overtime, is a mark of a truly great goaltender. He doesn't let things get to him. He plays the game the way he wants to play it. His April Fool's day battle with Patrick Roy says a lot of his competitiveness.

He was a WHL East Second-Team All-Star when he played with Brandon in the 1990-91 season.

He achieved his first two pro shutouts with the Adirondack Wings in 1992-93.

Chris recorded his first NHL victory against Los Angeles (8-3) in October of 1993.

He was named NHL Rookie Of The Month in February 1994 and had a 4-0 shutout in his first NHL playoff game. It was the first Detroit rookie shutout since 1951. Ozzie posted a .622 winning percentage as a rookie and his first two NHL shutouts were back-to-back.

During the 1995-96 season, Chris tied for first in the NHL for best goals against average (2.17), first in NHL wins (39), and tied for third in the league with 5 shutouts. With his teammate Mike Vernon, he earned the Jennings Trophy, for the fewest goals against in a regular season. He set a club record 21-game unbeaten streak in January-March 1996. His career best 13-game winning streak also set a new franchise record.

In his 100th career game in a win against Hartford he scored a goal, becoming the third goaltender in NHL history to be credited with scoring a goal. Ozzie played his first All-Star game in Boston in 1996. In the 1996-97 season, he , Vernon and Hodson, finished with the second best combined goals-against average (2.35) in the NHL. He also had an 8-game winning streak, six shutouts including a scoreless tie and was credited with an assist. His 1998 playoff performance in the crease resulted in 540 saves, 16 wins, 6 losses and one more Stanley Cup.

Chris is single and enjoys golf and tennis in his free time.

STATS		*SEASON*	*GP*	*W*	*L*	*T*	*GA*	*AVG*
WHL		1989-90	57	24	28	2	228	4.42
WHL		1990-91	46	23	18	3	173	3.95
WHL		1991-92	15	10	3	0	44	3.22
WHL			16	3	10	1	60	4.04
WHL			21	12	7	1	65	3.20
AHL		1992-93	45	19	19	4	159	3.91
NHL	DET	1993-94	41	23	8	5	105	2.86
AHL			4	3	1	1	13	3.26
AHL		1994-95	2	1	1	0	6	3.00
NHL	DET	1995	19	14	5	0	41	2.26
NHL	DET	1995-96	50	39	6	5	106	2.17
NHL	DET	1996-97	47	23	13	9	106	2.30
NHL	DET	1997-98	64	33	20	11	140	2.21

Chris Osgood

no. 31

<u>GOALIE</u>

6'0"

175 lbs

Catches Left

Born: Winnipeg, Manitoba

3.27.72

Last Amateur Club:

Sault Ste. Marie Greyhounds

Years Pro: 3

Acquired: Sign as free agent

in May 1993

Kevin is strong between the pipes. As Osgood's replacement last year, he went 9-3-3 with a 91.3 save percentage. His teammates called him Ticker when they found he had a heart problem in the past. But, he's healthy now and welcomes more time in the crease. Relaxed. Loose. Great reflexes. Comedian. His teammates love him. He's fun to be around.

Kevin played for three seasons as an amateur for the Sault Ste. Marie Greyhounds. He led in goals-against for all three seasons. He competed in three Memorial Cups with the Greyhounds and won it with them in 1993. He was named most valuable player in that victory.

Kevin joined the Adirondack Wings in 1993. He was named Rookie of the Year for the 1993-94 season.

He was signed by the Red Wings as a free agent in May 1993. He made is NHL debut at Pittsburgh on January 5, 1996. He played 28 minutes and allowed one goal. Ticker recorded his first NHL shutout in his first NHL start on January 6, 1996. It was a 2-0 victory (20 saves) over Chicago. He became the second Red Wing goalie in history to earn a shutout in his first regular season start.

He was 2-2-1 in the six games he played in 1996- 97 which included a shutout on December 4 against Washington. He registered his first assist on a power play goal on March 19 against Boston in a 4-1 victory.

Kevin and his wife Maarika live in Sault Ste. Marie in the off season where Kevin enjoys golf and fishing.

STATS

	SEASON	GP	W	L	T	GA	AVG
OHL	1990-91	30	18	11	0	88	3.22
OHL	1991-92	50	28	12	4	151	3.33
OHL	1992-93	26	18	5	2	76	3.10
IHL		14	5	9	0	53	4.09
AHL	1993-94	37	20	10	5	102	2.94
AHL	1994-95	51	19	22	8	161	3.54
NHL DET	1995-96	4	2	0	0	3	1.10
AHL		32	13	13	2	87	3.16
IHL	1996-97	2	1	1	0	7	3.54
NHL DET	1996-97	6	2	2	1	8	1.63
NHL DET	1997-98	21	9	3	3	44	2.67

Kevin Hodson

no. 33

CENTER

5'11'''

190 lbs

Shoots Left

Born: Toronto, ON

5.24.71

Last Amateur Club:

Ottawa 67s

Years Pro: 8

Acquired: Obtained 6.30.93

from Winnipeg

Kris Draper

Kris Draper is called Drapes by his teammates. Speed. Heart. Toughness. Upbeat. Positive. Kris is a team player all the way. He's a hard checker and a play wrecker. He plays hard every game, every period. He loves life, loves people and loves hockey.

He posted his career best last year, in goals(13), assists(10) and points(23). But the biggest goal of his career came at 15:24 overtime in Game 2 of the Stanley Cup Finals. Lapointe stole the puck and made a replay perfect pass to Kris who one-timed it passed Olie the Goalie for a 5-4 victory in the most exciting game of the play-offs. Drapes emerged as a true overtime hero.

Kris played two seasons for the Canadian National Team and began his NHL career with Winnipeg in 1989. He became a Red Wing on June 30, 1993.

Back in 1995, Kris had another dramatic game-winning goal, against Chicago in the third period with 1:45 remaining to give the Red Wings a 3-2 victory en route to winning the Conference Championship.

In April 1996, he posted a career-high four-game point streak which included two game-winning assists. In the 1996-97 season, Kris scored eight goals during the regular season, and assisted on one shorthanded goal, scored one power play goal, two other goals and a game-winning assist during the first playoff round against St. Louis. He contributed a short-handed assist in the Stanley Cup Finals series against Philadelphia.

Off the ice, Kris Draper is a very sincere, honest and open person. He is very positive and pleasant to be around. Kris is a newlywed and usually spends his off-seasons in Ontario where he enjoys golf and mountain biking.

STATS

		SEASON	GP	G	A	PTS	PM
CDN	NAT'L	1988-89	60	11	15	26	16
CDN	NAT'L	1989-90	61	12	22	34	44
NHL	WIN	1990-91	3	1	0	1	5
AHL			39	19	42	61	35
NHL	WIN	1991-92	10	2	0	2	2
AHL			61	11	18	29	113
AHL		1992-93	67	12	23	35	40
NHL	WIN		7	0	0	0	2
AHL		1993-94	46	20	23	43	49
NHL	DET		39	5	8	13	31
NHL	DET	1995	36	2	6	8	22
NHL	DET	1995-96	52	7	9	16	32
NHL	DET	1996-97	76	8	5	13	73
NHL	DET	1997-98	64	13	10	23	45

no. 34

DEFENSE

6'1"
193 lbs
Shoots Left
Born: Newmarket, ON
8.17.61
Last Amateur Club:
Ohio State University Buckeyes
(CCHA)
Years Pro: 16
Acquired: Obtained from
Toronto 3.24.98

Jamie is not a flashy hockey player. He does whatever the coaches tell him to do. He will get the job done. Experienced. Compliant. Formidable. Aggressive. Dedicated. *Cooner* makes his presence felt by the opponents. He's a bump and grind blueliner who can bang the boards with anyone...and often does.

While playing for Toronto in November 1996, he picked up 20 penalty minutes in one period. He also tied the team record for most penalty minutes in one game.

In 1983-84, Jamie was named to the NHL All Rookie Team. He captured a silver medal as a member of Team Canada in the 1985 World Championships. He played in 22 playoff games when the Calgary Flames defeated the Montreal Canadiens for the Stanley Cup in 1989. He recorded a plus-29 in the 1990-91 season and played for Team Canada in World Hockey Tournament. He was nominated to the Second All-Star Team and was named the Tournament's top defenseman.

He has played in 1059 games in his career, scored 75 goals, 272 assists and 347 points. He played in 7 regular season games with the Red Wings in 1997-98 and contributed 7 assists. In the 1998 playoffs, he scored 2 game-winning goals. One goal in game 4 against Phoenix and another in game 3 against Dallas.

Jamie and his wife Karin have a son Colin and a daughter Kali. In the off season he spends quality time with his family and has been involved with the Canadian Cancer Society.

STATS

		SEASON	GP	G	A	PTS	PM
NHL	CAL	1986-87	79	7	33	40	111
Injured		1987-88	*	*	*	*	*
NHL	CAL	1988-89	72	8	19	27	76
NHL	CAL	1989-90	78	8	27	35	70
NHL	CAL	1990-91	79	7	15	22	84
NHL	CAL	1991-92	37	2	12	14	53
NHL	TOR		39	3	13	16	18
NHL	TOR	1992-93	77	4	15	19	55
NHL	TOR	1993-94	82	3	27	30	115
NHL	TOR	1995	46	2	8	10	75
NHL	TOR	1995-96	82	0	8	8	87
NHL	TOR	1996-97	73	1	10	11	93
NHL	TOR	1997-98	67	0	7	7	63
NHL	DET		7	0	0	0	2

Jamie Macoun

no. 38

GOALIE

5'8"

195 lbs

Catches Left

Born: Belleville, ON

10.2.74

Last Amateur Club:

Saskatoon

Years Pro: 2

Acquired:

6th Choice. 126th Overall

in the 1993 Entry Draft

Norm has to follow in some pretty big footsteps in the Red Wings crease. All indications are that he is ready, willing and able to do just that. Quick. Talented. Great reflexes. Competitive. Ambitious. He's ready to earn his place in the big league.

Although he has had less than three hours of ice time between the pipes for the Red Wings last season, he is credited with two wins and one tie in 4 games played, and a goals-against average of 2.02.

For the Adirondack Wings in 1997-98, he recorded 49 saves (24 in the 3rd period) in a 2-1 victory against Albany. He also established a new franchise record with 62 saves in a 3-2 overtime victory over Albany. He had a scoreless streak of 132 minutes, 12 seconds. He posted a 21-save shutout at Rochester, but did not win the game. It was the first 0-0 tie in Adirondack history. He also became the first Adirondack goaltender to register three 20 victory seasons. He was the starting goalie for Team Canada in the 1997-98 AHL All-Star Classic. He finished off the season with a new franchise single-season record for saves with 1890.

A year earlier, Norm established 17 Adirondack goaltending records. He also was selected AHL goaltender of the month, AHL Player of the Week twice, and led the AHL in games (68), wins (34) and minutes (3843).

He made his NHL debut on March 4, 1998 against Philadelphia. He stopped both shots he faced in 15 minutes of relief duty for Chris Osgood. He recorded 28 saves in his first NHL start in a 4-3 victory over Edmonton.

STATS

		SEASON	GP	W	L	T	GA	AVG
WHL		1991-92	29	13	6	3	87	3.41
WHL		1992-93	53	27	18	3	160	3.27
WHL		1993-94	56	41	13	1	148	2.76
AHL		1994-95	39	12	15	2	119	3.57
AHL		1995-96	54	24	18	6	135	2.75
AHL		1996-97	68	34	22	9	173	2.70
AHL		1997-98	66	27	29	8	190	3.07
NHL	DET	1998	4	2	0	1	6	2.02

Norm Maracle

no. 41

LEFT WING

5’11”

180 lbs

Shoots Left

Born: Moose Jaw, Saskatchewan

4.3.67

Last Amateur Club:

Spokane (WHL)

Years Pro: 10

Acquired: Signed as free agent

7.8.97

Brent Gilchrist

Brent missed the last six weeks of the regular season and most of the playoffs because of a groin injury. He fought through multiple injuries to keep playing. His teammates call him Gilly. Battler. Leader. Intelligent. Very physical. Extremely tough.

In spite of his injuries, he had 13 goals and 14 assists for 27 points and contributed 2 goals and 1 assist in the playoffs.

Brent was originally drafted by Montreal in the 1985 entry Draft but didn't play his first NHL game until 1988. He finished fifth in team scoring for Montreal in 1991-92 and established his own single season highs in goals(23), assists(27), points(50) and penalty minutes(57). Dallas acquired Brent in 1993 and he recorded two points in eight games. During the 1994-95 season he scored two multi-goal games and tied for third in the NHL in shorthanded goals with three. The 1995-96 season saw Brent recorded his second highest point total(42) of his career. He was tied for third on the team in goals and fourth in points. During the 1996-97 season, he scored 10 goals with 20 assists. He also scored two power play goals and two game winning goals that year and another 2 goals and two assists in the playoffs for Dallas.

Gilly signed with the Red Wings in July of 1997 as a free agent. His versatility, toughness and heart has helped the Wings to the championship.

He and his wife have two sons and spend the off- season in western Canada, where Brent likes to water ski, play golf and play tennis.

STATS

		SEASON	GP	G	A	PTS	PM
AHL		1987-88	77	26	48	74	83
NHL	MON	1988-89	49	8	16	24	16
AHL			7	6	5	11	7
NHL	MON	1989-90	57	9	15	24	28
NHL	MON	1990-91	51	6	9	15	10
NHL	MON	1991-92	79	23	27	50	57
NHL	EDM	1992-93	60	10	10	20	47
NHL	MIN		8	0	1	1	2
NHL	DAL	1993-94	76	17	14	31	31
NHL	DAL	1995	32	9	4	13	16
NHL	DAL	1995-96	77	20	22	42	36
NHL	DAL	1996-97	67	10	20	30	24
NHL	DET	1997-98	61	13	14	27	40

no. 44

Defense

6'3"

220 lbs

Shoots Left

Born: Bollnas, Swenden

1.9.75

Last Amateur Club:

MoDo (Sweden)

Years Pro: 3

Acquired: 1st choice,

22nd overall in 1993 Draft

Anders has earned a regular spot on the Blue Line. Talented. Poised. Great vision of the ice. Great passer. He tied with Uwe Krupp for 14th place in the league with a +21 rating. He contributed 7 goals and 14 assists for 21 points last season. He keeps learning and getting better with every game. His Red Wing teammates call him Andy. His opponents call him trouble.

Anders exhibited his exceptional hockey talents when he was just 15 years old. He won the Lill Strimmas scholarship as a top defenseman and he was voted Best Junior in his home country of Sweden in 1994. He played defense for the MoDo Swedish Amateur Club from 1992 through 1995. He played on the Swedish National Team and won the 1992 European Championship. He followed that with a silver medal win in the 1993 World Junior Championships.

Anders joined the Adirondack Wings in 1995. He led the team's defensemen in points(42) and was sixth overall in team scoring. Andy made his NHL debut in April of 1996 against Dallas. He appeared in his first NHL playoff game on May 23 in Colorado.

During the 1996-97 season , he finished with the second-best plus-minus (+10) and was third in scoring among Adirondack Wing defensemen.

He scored his first career playoff point against Phoenix in Game two on a power play. He added four more playoff assists to help his Red Wing team keep the Cup.

Anders is single and spends the off-season in his hometown of Bollnas, Sweden, where he enjoys golf.

STATS

		SEASON	GP	G	A	PTS	PM
SWEDEN		1992-93	20	0	2	2	2
SWEDEN		1993-94	38	2	8	10	42
SWEDEN		1994-95	39	3	6	9	54
AHL		1995-96	75	6	36	42	64
NHL	DET		1	0	0	0	2
AHL		1996-97	44	3	25	28	36
NHL	DET	1996-97	23	0	6	6	10
NHL	DET	1997-98	66	7	14	21	32

Anders Eriksson

no. 55

DEFENSE

6'2"

215 lbs

Shoots Right

Born: Scarborough, ON

12.21.61

Last Amateur Club:

Peterborough (OHL)

Years Pro: 17

Acquired: Obtained 3.18.97 from Toronto for future considerations

Larry Murphy now has 4 Stanley Cup rings. He was the experienced veteran the Wings needed in their quest for a Stanley repeat. Big. Slow. Underrated. Smart. Murph has veins of ice which his Blue Line buddy, Lidstrom can attest to. He's always open for an outlet pass. Always a threat. He's super strong on the power play. He is a future Hall of Famer. In fact, with career totals of 256 goals, 838 assists, 1103 points he's ahead of Bobby Orr and still counting.

Larry was originally drafted into the NHL by Los Angeles in 1980. His nearly two decades of experience saw him also play for Washington, Minnesota, Pittsburgh and Toronto before becoming a Red Wing.

In March 1996, he became one of only four defensemen in the history of the NHL to reach 1000 career points, trailing only Paul Coffey, Ray Bourque and Denis Potvin. In his 1994-95 season with Pittsburgh, he was named to the NHL second All-Star Team for the third time in his career. He also registered a nine-game point streak and a five-game assist streak that were the NHL's longest of the post season.

Murph has played in 14 consecutive Stanley Cup Playoffs. In the 1997 playoffs with the Red Wings, he finished tied for third in points among NHL defensemen, assisted on two game-winning goals and was plus-10 in the Stanley Cup Finals against Philadelphia. In the 1998 playoffs, he scored 15 points with 3 goals and 12 assists. He finished the regular season fourth among NHL defensemen in total points (52). He had the highest plus/minus rating on the club (plus 35). He was the only Red Wing to play an entire 82-game schedule.

Off the ice Larry watches the Stock Market religiously. He and his wife, Nancy have two daughters and one son, and spend the off-season near Toronto.

STATS

		SEASON	GP	G	A	PTS	PM
NHL	WASH	1987-88	79	8	53	61	72
NHL	WASH	1988-89	65	7	29	36	70
NHL	MIN		13	4	6	10	12
NHL	MIN	1989-90	77	10	58	68	44
NHL	MIN	1990-91	31	4	11	15	38
NHL	PIT		44	5	23	28	30
NHL	PIT	1991-92	77	21	56	77	48
NHL	PIT	1992-93	83	22	63	85	73
NHL	PIT	1993-94	84	17	56	73	44
NHL	PIT	1995	48	13	25	38	18
NHL	TOR	1995-96	82	12	49	61	34
NHL	TOR	1996-97	69	7	32	39	20
NHL	DET		12	2	4	6	0
NHL	DET	1997-98	82	11	41	52	37

Larry Murphy

no. 91

CENTER

6'2"
200lbs
Shoots Left
Born: Pskov, Russia
12.13.69
Last Amateur Club:
Central Red Army
(USSR)
Years Pro: 8
Acquired: 4th choice,
74th overall in
1989 entry Draft

Sergei is probably the most talented player on the most talented team in NHL hockey today. Superstar. Goal Scorer. Playmaker. He breathes hockey with every breath. He thinks hockey with every thought. He personifies hockey with every move ... on offense and defense. His teammates sometimes call him, The Surge ... because he , so often, provides the momentum that can change the outcome of a game.

After his 59 game hiatus last season, he returned to The Joe amidst almost deafening boos from Hockeytown fans. He scored only 6 goals and 11 assists in 21 regular season games. But in the post season when superstars are supposed to shine ... his performance was blinding. He scored a league-leading 10 goals in the playoffs. Before joining Detroit in July of 1990, Sergei played on the Central Red Army team and helped the Soviet national team to win gold medals in the 1989 and 1990 World Championships. He made the 1990-91 All Rookie Team and was voted second for the Calder Trophy.

In the 1993-94 season, Sergei equaled his personal best in power play goals(13), while setting his career highs in goals, assists, plus-minus and game-winning goals(10). He also became the sixth Red Wing to score a 50 goal season and the third center to score 100 points or more. He was third highest goal scorer in the NHL and second in total points. He also won the Hart trophy as the league's Most Valuable Player, the Selke trophy as the best defensive forward and the Lester B. Pearson award as the NHL's top performer. He was named Player of the Year by The Hockey News, the Sporting News and Hockey Digest.

In 1995, Sergei was the NHL post season leader in total points and assists in the 1995-96 season. He was also the club leader in points, goals and assists for the entire season.

He set the club record for most game-winning goals in a season and finished second in the NHL for game-winning goals. He also recorded two, 5-point performances and tallied his 500th career point.

In one game, he scored 5 goals, including the game-winning goal in overtime as his team beat Washington 5-4. His Russian teammate, Vladimir Konstantinov gave him 4 assists in that December victory.

As awesome as he is in competition, off the ice he is quiet and soft-spoken. You have to listen hard for a hint of a Russian accent. He is single and lives in suburban Detroit. He enjoys golf, boating, movies and travel.

STATS

		SEASON	GP	G	A	PTS	PM
CSKA		1986-87	29	6	6	12	12
CSKA		1987-88	48	7	9	16	20
CSKA		1988-89	44	9	8	17	35
CSKA		1989-90	48	19	10	29	10
NHL	DET	1990-91	77	31	48	79	66
NHL	DET	1991-92	80	32	54	86	72
NHL	DET	1992-93	73	34	53	87	72
NHL	DET	1993-94	82	56	64	120	34
NHL	DET	1995	42	20	30	50	24
NHL	DET	1995-96	78	39	68	107	48
NHL	DET	1996-97	74	30	33	63	30
NHL	DET	1997-98	21	6	11	17	25

Sergei Fedorov

no. 96

<u>LEFT WING</u>

6'0"

198 lbs

Shoots Left

Born: Pitea, Sweden, 1.23.73

Last Amateur Club: Lulea (Sweden)

Years Pro: 2

Acquired: 9th choice, 257th overall in 1994 Draft

Tomas Holmstrom

Tomas Holmstrom is the Red Wings' rising star and a playoff hero with 7 goals and 12 assists. Tough. Spunky. Feisty. Determined. His missing tooth on a smiling face is a familiar sight in front of the goal crease. Opponents whack him with a stick, he smiles. Whack him harder, he smiles more. But, he doesn't give an inch of ice. He just waits in front of the crease for his linemates to shoot.

Holmer is a scrapper and always a major headache for the other team. He is aggravating to play against and a growing scoring threat.

As an amateur player in Lulea, Sweden, he scored 26 goals, 25 assist for 51 points in 74 games played. He made his NHL debut as a Red Wing in the 1996-97 season opener at New Jersey. He scored his first NHL point on November 16th on a power play goal against San Jose. He was assigned to the Adirondack Wings December 30th. There, he scored 3 goals and one assist before being recalled January 13 back to the Red Wings. He played in his first playoff game April 16th against St. Louis and shared in the Red Wings 1997 Stanley Cup Championship.

In the 1998 march to keep the Cup in Hockeytown, Tomas played inspired team hockey, with 4 game-winning goals and a total of 19 points.

On the ice, he is pesky, irritating and aggravating. Off the ice, he is a lot of fun. He enjoys life and loves to laugh. He is still learning the American culture and the language still gives him problems.

During the off-season he likes to return to native Sweden.

STATS

	SEASON	G	G	A	PTS	PM
SWEDEN	1994-95	40	14	14	28	56
SWEDEN	1995-96	34	12	11	23	78
AHL	1996-97	6	3	1	4	7
NHL DET	1996-97	47	6	3	9	33
NHL DET	1997-98	57	5	17	22	44

PLAYOFF WRAP UP

SERIES 1 **Detroit vs. Phoenix**

Game 1	Detroit 6 Phoenix 3
Game 2	Phoenix 7 Detroit 4
Game 3	Phoenix 3 Detroit 2
Game 4	Detroit 4 Phoenix 2
Game 5	Detroit 3 Phoenix 1
Game 6	Detroit 5 Phoenix 2

The Detroit Red Wings win the series 4 games to 2

SERIES 2 **Detroit vs. St. Louis**

Game 1	St. Louis 4 Detroit 2
Game 2	Detroit 6 St. Louis 1
Game 3	Detroit 3 St. Louis 2 (OT goal by Shanahan)
Game 4	Detroit 5 St. Louis 2
Game 5	St. Louis 3 Detroit 1
Game 6	Detroit 6 St. Louis 1

Detroit moves to the next round defeating St. Louis 4 games to 2

Budweiser

18
ZA!PIZZA!

ERIKSSON
44
A
14

SERIES 3

Detroit vs. Dallas

Game 1 Detroit 2 Dallas 0
Game 2 Dallas 3 Detroit 1
Game 3 Detroit 5 Dallas 3
Game 4 Detroit 3 Dallas 2
Game 5 Dallas 3 Detroit 2
(OT goal by Langenbrunner)
Game 6 Detroit 2 Dallas 0
Detroit eliminates Dallas in the Western Conference Championship, 4 games to 2.

STANLEY CUP FINALS

Detroit vs. Washington

Game 1 Detroit 2 Washington 1
Game 2 Detroit 5 Washington 4
(OT goal by Draper)
Game 3 Detroit 2 Washington 1
Game 4 Detroit 4 Washington 1
Sweet Repeat. Detroit over Washington in 4 straight!

Stanley Stays in Hockeytown

The 1997 Stanley Cup was for the team, the city and the Hockeytown fans that had waited more than four decades for its arrival.

The 1998 Stanley Cup was different. This one was for Vladimir Konstantinov and Sergei Mnatsakanov, two Red Wing teammates who faced far greater challenges than keeping the Cup in Hockeytown.

Although the players and coaches never talked about it in the locker room, thoughts of the Vladinator and Sergei were always with them. Each time a player put on his gear to play a game, or passed by Vlady's equipment stall, or the training room where the team's masseur used to be, he felt something inside.

Each player felt something a little different, yet the same. It was like an invisible aura that enveloped each player, each coach, every member of the Red Wing organization. It united them, motivated them to maybe skate a little faster, hit a little harder, dig a little deeper. They became a team with a mission, a mission to win it all for their missing teammates, a mission to keep Stanley here, in Hockeytown.

From the very first day at training camp, there was little doubt that the silver chalice that everyone had waited so long for, fought so hard for ... should stay, must stay, would stay in Hockeytown. The team played inspired hockey throughout the regular season and the playoffs. Everyone could sense it ... the players, the coaches, the fans ... and the opponents. Vlady and Sergei were on the ice, with their teammates, for each series, every game, every period, every play.

And on the final play with seconds to go, Larry Murphy skated with the puck to the left side of the Red Wings goal, as the buzzer sounded and gloves, sticks and fans reached for the ceiling. The Red Wings had done it. A repeat. Back-to-back sweeps. The Red Wings won the Cup, again. Only this time, it was 52 weeks between Cups...not 42 years.

When the playoff MVP, Steve Yzerman presented the Cup to Vlady in his wheel-chair, on the ice with his ecstatic teammates surrounding him, and Vlady raised his two fingers in victory symbolizing back-to-back cups, there was not a dry eye in Hockeytown.

GET INSIDE!

inside HOCKEYTOWN™

Learn about the Stanley Cup Champions throughout the 1998-99 season, with your subscription to "Inside Hockeytown"

7 ISSUES ONLY $28

1-313-396-7575

Price subject to change • Canadian Subscriptions $34 • International Subscriptions $63

MOST WANTED

These posters are wanted by everyone. Fans. Customers. Targeted demographics. Because, that's what we do at CFW Creative Sports. We Create advertising and Merchandising that appeals to the masses, that communicate effective selling messages for our clients. Effective marketing that produces measurable results.

But, we don't just do posters. We also do brochures, catalogs, merchandising and much more. But, they all have one thing in common... they *are* wanted.

Now, if you *want* advertising and marketing that works. Just give us a call... if you *want* to.

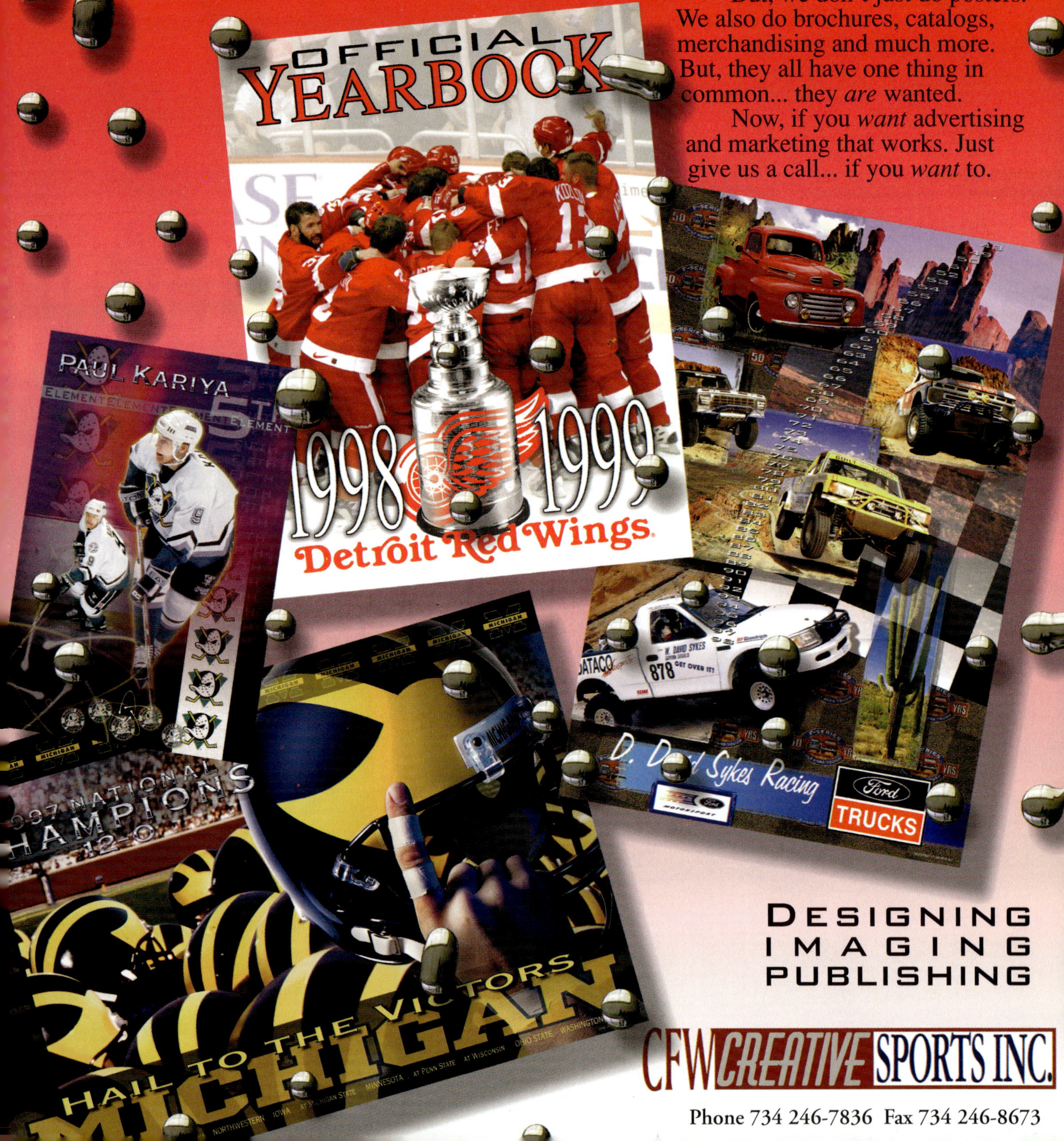

DESIGNING
IMAGING
PUBLISHING

CFW CREATIVE SPORTS INC.

Phone 734 246-7836 Fax 734 246-8673

1998-99 SCHEDULE

OCT	Sat	10	@ Toronto	7:00 p.m.
	Tue	13	@ Washington	7:30 p.m.
	Fri	16	ST. LOUIS	8:00 p.m.
	Sun	18	CALGARY	3:00 p.m.
	Wed	21	NASHVILLE	7:30 p.m.
	Fri	23	TORONTO	7:30 p.m.
	Sat	24	@ Montreal	7:00 p.m.
	Wed	28	@ Florida	7:30 p.m.
	Thu	29	@ St. Louis	8:00 p.m.
	Sat	31	@ Dallas	8:00 p.m.
NOV	Tue	3	CALGARY	7:30 p.m.
	Fri	6	@ Phoenix	9:00 p.m.
	Sun	8	@ Anaheim	8:00 p.m.
	Wed	11	ST. LOUIS	7:30 p.m.
	Fri	13	DALLAS	7:30 p.m.
	Mon	16	@ Calgary	9:00 p.m.
	Wed	18	@ Edmonton	9:00 p.m.
	Sat	21	@ Vancouver	10:00 p.m.
	Wed	25	ANAHEIM	7:30 p.m.
	Fri	27	VANCOUVER	7:30 p.m.
	Sun	29	San Jose	3:00 p.m.
DEC	Wed	2	@ Colorado	9:00 p.m.
	Fri	4	@ San Jose	10:30 p.m.
	Sat	5	@ Los Angeles	10:30 p.m.
	Tue	8	CHICAGO	7:30 p.m.
	Fri	11	EDMONTON	7:30 p.m.
	Sat	12	@ Carolina	7:00 p.m.
	Wed	16	BOSTON	7:30 p.m.
	Fri	18	DALLAS	7:30 p.m.
	Sat	19	@ Boston	7:30 p.m.
	Tue	22	PHOENIX	7:30 p.m.
	Wed	23	@ Nashville	8:00 p.m.
	Sat	26	@ St. Louis	8:00 p.m.
	Mon	28	ST. LOUIS	7:00 p.m.
	Thur	31	TORONTO	7:30 p.m.
JAN	Sat	2	CHICAGO	1:00 p.m.
	Sun	3	@ Chicago	8:00 p.m.
	Wed	6	OTTAWA	7:30 p.m.
	Sat	9	COLORADO	1:00 p.m.
	Sun	10	@ Ottawa	2:00 p.m.
	Tue	13	MONTREAL	7:30 p.m.
	Thu	14	NASHVILLE	7:30 p.m.
	Sat	16	@ Vancouver	10:00 p.m.
	Sun	17	@ Edmonton	8:00 p.m.
	Tue	19	@ Calgary	9:00 p.m.
	Thu	21	CAROLINA	7:00 p.m.
	Tue	26	@ Nashville	8:00 p.m.
	Sat	30	NY RANGERS	7:30 p.m.
FEB	Mon	1	@ New Jersey	7:30 p.m.
	Wed	3	NY ISLANDERS	7:30 p.m.
	Fri	5	COLORADO	7:30 p.m.
	Sun	7	@ Pittsburgh	3:00 p.m.
	Tue	9	@ Nashville	8:00 p.m.
	Thu	11	EDMONTON	7:30 p.m.
	Fri	12	@ Chicago	8:30 p.m.
	Sun	14	@ NY Rangers	3:00 p.m.
	Wed	17	SAN JOSE	7:30 p.m.
	Fri	19	NEW JERSEY	7:30 p.m.
	Sun	21	@ Buffalo	3:00 p.m.
	Wed	24	LOS ANGLES	7:30 p.m.
	Fri	26	FLORIDA	7:30 p.m.
	Sat	27	@ NY Rangers	7:00 p.m.
MAR	Fri	5	@ Phoenix	9:00 p.m.
	Sun	7	@ Anaheim	8:00 p.m.
	Tues	9	@ Los Angeles	10:30 p.m.
	Fri	12	@ San Jose	10:30 p.m.
	Sun	14	@ Colorado	3:00 p.m.
	Wed	17	PHOENIX	7:30 p.m.
	Fri	19	@ Tampa Bay	7:30 p.m.
	Sun	21	@ Philadelphia	3:00 p.m.
	Wed	24	BUFFALO	7:30 p.m.
	Fri	26	TAMPA BAY	7:30 p.m.
	Sun	28	PHILADELPHIA	3:00 p.m.
	Wed	31	LOS ANGELES	7:30 p.m.
APR	Fri	2	CHICAGO	7:30 p.m.
	Sun	4	@ Dallas	3:00 p.m.
	Mon	5	ANAHEIM	7:30 p.m.
	Wed	7	VANCOUVER	7:30 p.m.
	Fri	9	@ St. Louis	7:30 p.m.
	Sun	11	PITTSBURGH	3:00 p.m.
	Wed	14	NASHVILLE	7:30 p.m.
	Sat	17	@ Chicago	7:30 p.m.

ALL TIMES ARE EASTERN STANDARD TIME - HOME GAMES IN CAPS

IN THE WINGS

PHILIPPE
AUDET
Left Wing
6'2"
175 lbs.
Shoots Left
Born: Ottawa, Ontario
6.4.77
Last Amateur Club:
Granby

RYAN
BACH
Goalie
6'1"
175 lbs.
Catches Left
Born: Sherwood Park,
Alberta 10.21.73
Last Amateur Club:
Houston (IHL)

JASON
ELLIOTT
Goalie
6'2"
183 lbs.
Catches Left
Born: Inovik, Northwest
Territories 11/10/75
Last Amateur Club:
Cornell (ECAC)

MAXIM KUZNETSOV

Defense
6'5"
198lbs.
Shoots Left
Born: Pavlodar, Russia 3.24.77
Last Amateur Club: Adirondack (AHL)

DARRYL LAPLANTE

Center
6'1"
185 lbs.
Shoots Left
Born: Calgary, Alberta 3.28.77
Last Amateur Club: Adirondack (AHL)

AREN MILLER

Goalie
6'2"
208 lbs.
Catches Left
Born: Oxbow, Saskatchewan 1.13.78
Last Amateur Club: Spokane (WHL)

BARRY POTOMSKI

Left Wing
6'2"
215 lbs.
Shoots Left
Born: Windsor, Ontario 11.24.72
Last Amateur Club: Las Vegas (IHL)

STACY ROEST

Center
5'9"
192 lbs.
Shoots Right
Born: Lethbridge, Alberta 3.15.74
Last Amateur Club: Medicine Hat (WHL)

JESSE WALLIN

Defense
6'2"
190 lbs.
Shoots Left
Born: Saskatoon, Saskatchewan 1.13.78
Last Amateur Club: Red Deer (WHL)